50 Premium International Chicken Dishes

By: Kelly Johnson

Table of Contents

- Chicken Parmesan (Italy)
- Butter Chicken (India)
- Chicken Cacciatore (Italy)
- Coq au Vin (France)
- Chicken Shawarma (Middle East)
- Pollo Asado (Mexico)
- Chicken Kiev (Ukraine)
- Tandoori Chicken (India)
- Chicken Satay with Peanut Sauce (Indonesia)
- Chicken and Mushroom Stroganoff (Russia)
- Chicken Tagine with Apricots (Morocco)
- Arroz con Pollo (Latin America)
- Chicken Biryani (India)
- Chicken Schnitzel (Germany)
- Chicken Fricassée (France)
- General Tso's Chicken (China)
- Jerk Chicken (Jamaica)
- Pollo al Ajillo (Spain)
- Hainanese Chicken Rice (Singapore)
- Thai Green Curry Chicken (Thailand)
- Chicken Fajitas (Mexico)
- Chicken Alfredo (Italy)
- Chicken Mole (Mexico)
- Peruvian Roast Chicken (Peru)
- Chicken Paprikash (Hungary)
- Chicken Souvlaki (Greece)
- Baked Chicken with Lemon and Herbs (France)
- Chicken Korma (India)
- Kung Pao Chicken (China)
- Chicken Piri Piri (Portugal)
- Chicken Pot Pie (USA)
- Chicken Empanadas (Argentina)
- Chicken Schnitzel (Austria)
- Chicken Satay (Malaysia)
- Chicken Enchiladas (Mexico)

- Chicken Piccata (Italy)
- Chicken Rendang (Indonesia)
- Chicken Caesar Salad (USA)
- Poulet Roti (France)
- Khao Man Gai (Thailand)
- Spicy Chicken Wings (Korea)
- Chicken Paella (Spain)
- Chicken Adobo (Philippines)
- Chicken Burritos (Mexico)
- Chicken Vindaloo (India)
- Chicken and Chorizo Paella (Spain)
- Stuffed Chicken with Spinach and Feta (Greece)
- Cacciatore di Pollo (Italy)
- Grilled Peri Peri Chicken (South Africa)
- Chicken Szechuan (China)

Chicken Parmesan (Italy)

Ingredients:

- 4 boneless, skinless chicken breasts
- 1 cup all-purpose flour
- 2 large eggs, beaten
- 1 cup breadcrumbs
- 1/2 cup grated Parmesan cheese
- 2 cups marinara sauce
- 2 cups shredded mozzarella cheese
- Fresh basil leaves (optional)
- Olive oil, for frying
- Salt and pepper, to taste

Instructions:

1. Preheat oven to 375°F (190°C).
2. Season chicken breasts with salt and pepper. Dredge in flour, then dip in eggs, and coat in a mixture of breadcrumbs and Parmesan cheese.
3. Heat olive oil in a skillet over medium-high heat. Fry chicken for 3-4 minutes on each side until golden.
4. Place chicken in a baking dish, top with marinara sauce and mozzarella cheese. Bake for 20-25 minutes until the chicken is cooked through and the cheese is melted.
5. Garnish with fresh basil and serve hot with pasta or a side salad.

Butter Chicken (India)

Ingredients:

- 1 lb chicken breast or thighs, cut into pieces
- 2 tablespoons butter
- 1 onion, finely chopped
- 3 cloves garlic, minced
- 1-inch piece ginger, minced
- 1 can (14 oz) tomato puree
- 1/2 cup heavy cream
- 1 tablespoon garam masala
- 1 teaspoon ground cumin
- 1 teaspoon ground coriander
- 1 teaspoon turmeric
- Salt and pepper, to taste
- Fresh cilantro, chopped (for garnish)

Instructions:

1. In a large skillet, melt butter and sauté onions, garlic, and ginger until fragrant.
2. Add the chicken pieces and cook until browned.
3. Stir in spices (garam masala, cumin, coriander, turmeric) and cook for another minute.
4. Add tomato puree, heavy cream, salt, and pepper. Simmer for 15-20 minutes, until the sauce thickens and chicken is tender.
5. Garnish with cilantro and serve with rice or naan.

Chicken Cacciatore (Italy)

Ingredients:

- 4 chicken thighs or breasts
- 1 onion, sliced
- 1 bell pepper, sliced
- 2 cloves garlic, minced
- 1 can (14 oz) diced tomatoes
- 1/2 cup dry white wine
- 1/4 cup chicken broth
- 1 teaspoon dried oregano
- 1 teaspoon dried basil
- 1/4 teaspoon red pepper flakes (optional)
- Olive oil, for cooking
- Salt and pepper, to taste

Instructions:

1. Heat olive oil in a large skillet over medium heat. Brown the chicken pieces on both sides, then set aside.
2. In the same skillet, sauté onions, bell pepper, and garlic until softened.
3. Add wine to deglaze the pan, scraping up any browned bits. Stir in tomatoes, chicken broth, oregano, basil, and red pepper flakes.
4. Return the chicken to the skillet. Cover and simmer for 30-40 minutes, until the chicken is tender.
5. Serve with pasta, rice, or crusty bread.

Coq au Vin (France)

Ingredients:

- 4 chicken thighs or a whole chicken, cut into parts
- 2 tablespoons olive oil
- 1 onion, chopped
- 2 carrots, sliced
- 3 cloves garlic, minced
- 2 cups red wine (preferably Burgundy)
- 1/2 cup chicken broth
- 1 bouquet garni (thyme, bay leaf, parsley)
- 1/2 lb small mushrooms, halved
- 1/4 cup pancetta or bacon, diced
- Salt and pepper, to taste

Instructions:

1. In a large Dutch oven, heat olive oil and brown the chicken pieces on all sides. Set aside.
2. In the same pot, sauté onions, carrots, garlic, and pancetta until softened.
3. Pour in wine, chicken broth, and add the bouquet garni. Stir to combine.
4. Return chicken to the pot and bring to a simmer. Cover and cook for 45 minutes.
5. Add mushrooms and cook for an additional 15 minutes until chicken is tender and sauce is reduced.
6. Remove bouquet garni, season with salt and pepper, and serve with potatoes or crusty bread.

Chicken Shawarma (Middle East)

Ingredients:

- 4 boneless chicken thighs, skin-on
- 3 tablespoons olive oil
- 3 cloves garlic, minced
- 1 teaspoon ground cumin
- 1 teaspoon paprika
- 1 teaspoon ground coriander
- 1 teaspoon turmeric
- 1/2 teaspoon ground cinnamon
- 1/4 teaspoon cayenne pepper (optional)
- Salt and pepper, to taste
- Pita bread or flatbread
- Tahini sauce or garlic sauce, for serving

Instructions:

1. In a bowl, mix olive oil, garlic, spices, salt, and pepper. Coat chicken thighs with the marinade and refrigerate for at least 2 hours (overnight for best results).
2. Preheat grill or skillet over medium-high heat. Grill chicken for 6-7 minutes on each side until fully cooked.
3. Slice chicken and serve in pita bread with tahini or garlic sauce, and salad ingredients like cucumber, tomatoes, and onions.

Pollo Asado (Mexico)

Ingredients:

- 4 bone-in chicken thighs or legs
- 1/4 cup orange juice
- 1/4 cup lime juice
- 2 cloves garlic, minced
- 1 tablespoon chili powder
- 1 teaspoon cumin
- 1 teaspoon oregano
- Salt and pepper, to taste

Instructions:

1. In a bowl, combine orange juice, lime juice, garlic, chili powder, cumin, oregano, salt, and pepper.
2. Marinate chicken in the mixture for at least 2 hours.
3. Preheat grill or skillet to medium heat. Cook chicken for 25-30 minutes, turning occasionally, until fully cooked and golden brown.
4. Serve with rice, beans, or tortillas.

Chicken Kiev (Ukraine)

Ingredients:

- 4 boneless, skinless chicken breasts
- 1/2 cup unsalted butter, softened
- 2 cloves garlic, minced
- 2 tablespoons fresh parsley, chopped
- 1 tablespoon fresh dill, chopped
- Salt and pepper, to taste
- 1/2 cup all-purpose flour
- 2 large eggs, beaten
- 1 cup breadcrumbs
- Vegetable oil, for frying

Instructions:

1. In a bowl, mix softened butter with garlic, parsley, dill, salt, and pepper. Roll into a log and refrigerate until firm.
2. Make a pocket in each chicken breast and stuff with the garlic herb butter. Seal the edges with toothpicks.
3. Dredge stuffed chicken in flour, dip in beaten eggs, and coat in breadcrumbs.
4. Heat oil in a skillet and fry chicken for 6-7 minutes per side until golden and cooked through.
5. Serve with mashed potatoes or steamed vegetables.

Tandoori Chicken (India)

Ingredients:

- 4 chicken thighs, skinless
- 1/2 cup plain yogurt
- 2 tablespoons lemon juice
- 1 tablespoon ground cumin
- 1 tablespoon ground coriander
- 1 tablespoon paprika
- 1 teaspoon turmeric
- 1 teaspoon ground ginger
- 2 cloves garlic, minced
- Salt and pepper, to taste

Instructions:

1. Mix yogurt, lemon juice, spices, garlic, salt, and pepper in a bowl. Coat chicken in the marinade and refrigerate for at least 2 hours.
2. Preheat grill or oven to 400°F (200°C). Grill chicken for 25-30 minutes until cooked through and slightly charred.
3. Serve with naan or rice and a side of cucumber raita.

Chicken Satay with Peanut Sauce (Indonesia)

Ingredients:

- 4 boneless, skinless chicken breasts, cut into strips
- 1/4 cup soy sauce
- 1 tablespoon brown sugar
- 2 tablespoons vegetable oil
- 1 clove garlic, minced
- 1 teaspoon ground coriander
- 1/2 teaspoon turmeric powder
- 1 tablespoon lime juice
- Bamboo skewers (soaked in water for 30 minutes)

For the Peanut Sauce:

- 1/2 cup peanut butter
- 2 tablespoons soy sauce
- 2 tablespoons lime juice
- 1 tablespoon brown sugar
- 1/4 cup coconut milk
- 1 clove garlic, minced
- 1 teaspoon ginger, grated
- Pinch of chili flakes (optional)

Instructions:

1. In a bowl, mix soy sauce, brown sugar, oil, garlic, coriander, turmeric, and lime juice. Add chicken strips and marinate for at least 30 minutes.
2. Thread the chicken onto soaked bamboo skewers. Preheat grill or skillet to medium-high heat.
3. Grill chicken for 3-4 minutes per side until cooked through.
4. In a small bowl, mix together all the peanut sauce ingredients until smooth.
5. Serve the chicken skewers with the peanut sauce for dipping.

Chicken and Mushroom Stroganoff (Russia)

Ingredients:

- 4 boneless, skinless chicken breasts, cut into strips
- 2 tablespoons butter
- 1 onion, finely chopped
- 2 cloves garlic, minced
- 8 oz mushrooms, sliced
- 1/2 cup chicken broth
- 1/2 cup sour cream
- 1 tablespoon Dijon mustard
- Salt and pepper, to taste
- Fresh parsley, chopped (for garnish)

Instructions:

1. In a skillet, melt butter over medium heat. Add onions and garlic and sauté until softened.
2. Add chicken strips and cook until browned on all sides.
3. Add mushrooms and cook until tender.
4. Stir in chicken broth, sour cream, mustard, salt, and pepper. Simmer for 10 minutes, until the sauce thickens and the chicken is cooked through.
5. Garnish with parsley and serve with egg noodles or rice.

Chicken Tagine with Apricots (Morocco)

Ingredients:

- 4 bone-in chicken thighs
- 2 tablespoons olive oil
- 1 onion, sliced
- 2 cloves garlic, minced
- 1 tablespoon ground cumin
- 1 teaspoon ground turmeric
- 1 teaspoon ground cinnamon
- 1/2 teaspoon ground ginger
- 1 cup chicken broth
- 1/2 cup dried apricots, halved
- 1/4 cup almonds, toasted (optional)
- Fresh cilantro, chopped (for garnish)

Instructions:

1. In a large Dutch oven or tagine pot, heat olive oil over medium-high heat. Brown chicken thighs on both sides and set aside.
2. In the same pot, sauté onion and garlic until softened.
3. Stir in cumin, turmeric, cinnamon, and ginger, and cook for 1-2 minutes.
4. Add chicken broth, apricots, and the browned chicken back into the pot. Bring to a simmer and cover.
5. Cook for 40-45 minutes, until chicken is tender. Garnish with almonds and cilantro before serving with couscous.

Arroz con Pollo (Latin America)

Ingredients:

- 4 chicken thighs, bone-in
- 2 tablespoons olive oil
- 1 onion, chopped
- 2 cloves garlic, minced
- 1 bell pepper, chopped
- 1 1/2 cups rice
- 1 1/2 cups chicken broth
- 1/2 cup peas
- 1 teaspoon ground cumin
- 1/2 teaspoon paprika
- Salt and pepper, to taste
- Fresh cilantro, chopped (for garnish)

Instructions:

1. Heat olive oil in a large skillet over medium heat. Brown the chicken thighs on both sides and set aside.
2. In the same skillet, sauté onions, garlic, and bell pepper until softened.
3. Add rice, cumin, paprika, salt, and pepper. Stir well to coat the rice in the spices.
4. Pour in chicken broth and bring to a simmer. Return chicken to the pan, cover, and cook for 30 minutes, or until rice is tender.
5. Add peas in the last 5 minutes of cooking. Garnish with cilantro and serve.

Chicken Biryani (India)

Ingredients:

- 4 bone-in chicken thighs or breasts
- 1 1/2 cups basmati rice
- 2 tablespoons ghee (or vegetable oil)
- 1 onion, sliced
- 2 cloves garlic, minced
- 1-inch piece ginger, minced
- 1 teaspoon ground cumin
- 1 teaspoon ground coriander
- 1 teaspoon garam masala
- 1/2 teaspoon ground turmeric
- 1/2 teaspoon chili powder
- 1/2 cup yogurt
- 1/4 cup cilantro, chopped
- 1/4 cup mint leaves, chopped
- Salt, to taste

Instructions:

1. In a large bowl, marinate chicken with yogurt, garlic, ginger, cumin, coriander, garam masala, turmeric, chili powder, and salt. Let sit for at least 1 hour.
2. Rinse basmati rice under cold water until water runs clear. Set aside.
3. In a large pot, heat ghee over medium heat. Sauté onions until golden brown, then remove half for garnish.
4. Add garlic and ginger to the pot, cook for 1 minute, then add marinated chicken. Cook for 10 minutes until browned.
5. Stir in rice and water (about 2 cups), cover, and cook on low for 20-25 minutes.
6. Garnish with fried onions, cilantro, and mint. Serve hot.

Chicken Schnitzel (Germany)

Ingredients:

- 4 boneless, skinless chicken breasts
- 1 cup all-purpose flour
- 2 large eggs, beaten
- 1 cup breadcrumbs
- 1/4 cup vegetable oil, for frying
- Lemon wedges (for serving)
- Salt and pepper, to taste

Instructions:

1. Season chicken breasts with salt and pepper. Place flour, eggs, and breadcrumbs in separate shallow bowls.
2. Dredge each piece of chicken in flour, dip into beaten eggs, and coat with breadcrumbs.
3. Heat oil in a large skillet over medium-high heat. Fry chicken for 3-4 minutes per side until golden brown and crispy.
4. Serve with lemon wedges and a side of mashed potatoes or a fresh salad.

Chicken Fricassée (France)

Ingredients:

- 4 chicken thighs, bone-in, skin removed
- 2 tablespoons butter
- 1 onion, chopped
- 2 carrots, sliced
- 1 cup white wine
- 1/2 cup chicken broth
- 1/2 cup heavy cream
- 1 teaspoon fresh thyme leaves
- Salt and pepper, to taste

Instructions:

1. In a large skillet, melt butter over medium heat. Brown chicken thighs on both sides and set aside.
2. In the same skillet, sauté onions and carrots until softened.
3. Add wine and chicken broth, scraping up any browned bits from the pan.
4. Return chicken to the skillet, cover, and simmer for 30-35 minutes, until chicken is cooked through.
5. Stir in heavy cream, thyme, salt, and pepper. Simmer for an additional 5 minutes. Serve hot with rice or potatoes.

General Tso's Chicken (China)

Ingredients:

- 4 boneless, skinless chicken breasts, cut into bite-sized pieces
- 1/2 cup cornstarch
- 2 tablespoons soy sauce
- 1 tablespoon rice vinegar
- 1 tablespoon hoisin sauce
- 1 tablespoon sugar
- 1/2 teaspoon crushed red pepper flakes
- 2 cloves garlic, minced
- 2 tablespoons vegetable oil
- Green onions, chopped (for garnish)

Instructions:

1. Coat chicken pieces in cornstarch and fry in hot oil until crispy. Remove from oil and set aside.
2. In a small bowl, whisk together soy sauce, rice vinegar, hoisin sauce, sugar, and red pepper flakes.
3. In the same skillet, sauté garlic until fragrant, then add sauce mixture and bring to a simmer.
4. Add crispy chicken to the skillet, toss to coat with sauce, and cook for 3-4 minutes until the sauce thickens.
5. Garnish with green onions and serve with steamed rice.

Jerk Chicken (Jamaica)

Ingredients:

- 4 bone-in chicken thighs or whole chicken
- 1/4 cup soy sauce
- 1/4 cup vegetable oil
- 2 tablespoons brown sugar
- 2 teaspoons ground allspice
- 1 teaspoon ground thyme
- 1 teaspoon cinnamon
- 1 tablespoon grated ginger
- 3 cloves garlic, minced
- 2-3 Scotch bonnet peppers (or habaneros), chopped
- 1/4 cup green onions, chopped
- 1/4 cup fresh lime juice
- Salt and pepper, to taste

Instructions:

1. In a blender or food processor, combine soy sauce, oil, brown sugar, allspice, thyme, cinnamon, ginger, garlic, Scotch bonnet peppers, green onions, lime juice, salt, and pepper. Blend until smooth.
2. Coat the chicken with the marinade, cover, and refrigerate for at least 2 hours (overnight is best).
3. Preheat your grill to medium heat. Grill chicken for 30-40 minutes, turning occasionally, until the chicken is cooked through and has a nice char.
4. Serve with rice and peas or grilled vegetables.

Pollo al Ajillo (Spain)

Ingredients:

- 4 bone-in chicken thighs or a whole chicken, cut into pieces
- 4 tablespoons olive oil
- 10 cloves garlic, peeled and smashed
- 1/2 cup dry white wine
- 1/4 cup chicken broth
- 1 teaspoon paprika
- 1 teaspoon fresh thyme leaves
- Salt and pepper, to taste
- Fresh parsley, chopped (for garnish)

Instructions:

1. Heat olive oil in a large skillet over medium heat. Season chicken with salt and pepper and brown on all sides, about 8-10 minutes.
2. Add garlic cloves and cook for another 2-3 minutes until fragrant, but be careful not to burn the garlic.
3. Stir in wine, chicken broth, paprika, and thyme. Bring to a simmer, cover, and cook for 25-30 minutes, until the chicken is tender and fully cooked.
4. Garnish with chopped parsley and serve with crusty bread or roasted potatoes.

Hainanese Chicken Rice (Singapore)

Ingredients:

- 1 whole chicken
- 5-6 slices of ginger
- 2 stalks green onions
- 4 cups jasmine rice
- 1 tablespoon sesame oil
- 1 tablespoon vegetable oil
- 1 cucumber, sliced (for garnish)
- Salt, to taste

For the sauce:

- 1/4 cup soy sauce
- 2 tablespoons chicken broth
- 1 tablespoon sesame oil
- 2 cloves garlic, minced
- 1 small chili (optional), chopped
- 1 tablespoon ginger, minced

Instructions:

1. Bring a large pot of water to a boil. Add the whole chicken, ginger, and green onions. Simmer for about 40 minutes, until the chicken is cooked through.
2. While the chicken is cooking, rinse rice under cold water. Cook rice with chicken stock (from the poaching pot) for added flavor.
3. After the chicken is cooked, remove it from the pot and rub with sesame oil. Let rest, then chop into pieces.
4. To make the sauce, combine soy sauce, chicken broth, sesame oil, garlic, chili, and ginger in a small pan and heat through for 2-3 minutes.
5. Serve the chicken over the rice with cucumber slices and drizzle with the sauce.

Thai Green Curry Chicken (Thailand)

Ingredients:

- 4 boneless, skinless chicken breasts, sliced
- 2 tablespoons green curry paste
- 1 can (14 oz) coconut milk
- 1 tablespoon fish sauce
- 1 tablespoon sugar
- 1 red bell pepper, sliced
- 1 zucchini, sliced
- 1/2 cup fresh basil leaves
- 1 tablespoon vegetable oil
- 1/2 cup chicken broth

Instructions:

1. Heat oil in a large pan over medium heat. Add the green curry paste and sauté for 1-2 minutes until fragrant.
2. Add chicken slices and cook until browned.
3. Stir in coconut milk, chicken broth, fish sauce, and sugar. Bring to a simmer and cook for 10-15 minutes until the chicken is fully cooked and the sauce thickens.
4. Add bell pepper, zucchini, and basil leaves. Cook for another 3-4 minutes until the vegetables are tender.
5. Serve with jasmine rice or noodles.

Chicken Fajitas (Mexico)

Ingredients:

- 4 boneless, skinless chicken breasts, sliced into strips
- 1 tablespoon olive oil
- 1 onion, sliced
- 1 bell pepper, sliced
- 1 teaspoon ground cumin
- 1 teaspoon chili powder
- 1/2 teaspoon smoked paprika
- 1/2 teaspoon garlic powder
- Salt and pepper, to taste
- Flour tortillas, for serving
- Lime wedges (for garnish)

Instructions:

1. Heat olive oil in a large skillet over medium heat. Add the chicken strips and cook until browned and cooked through, about 7-8 minutes.
2. Add sliced onion and bell pepper to the pan and cook until softened, about 5-6 minutes.
3. Sprinkle with cumin, chili powder, paprika, garlic powder, salt, and pepper. Toss to coat and cook for another 2 minutes.
4. Serve the chicken and vegetables in warm flour tortillas with a squeeze of lime.

Chicken Alfredo (Italy)

Ingredients:

- 4 boneless, skinless chicken breasts
- 2 tablespoons olive oil
- 3 cloves garlic, minced
- 1 cup heavy cream
- 1 cup grated Parmesan cheese
- 1/2 teaspoon Italian seasoning
- 1 tablespoon fresh parsley, chopped
- 1 pound fettuccine pasta
- Salt and pepper, to taste

Instructions:

1. Cook the fettuccine pasta according to package directions and set aside.
2. In a large skillet, heat olive oil over medium heat. Season chicken breasts with salt and pepper and cook for 6-7 minutes on each side, until browned and cooked through. Remove and set aside.
3. In the same skillet, sauté garlic until fragrant, about 1 minute. Add heavy cream and bring to a simmer.
4. Stir in Parmesan cheese and Italian seasoning, then cook for another 3-4 minutes until the sauce thickens.
5. Slice the chicken and add it to the sauce. Serve over the fettuccine pasta and garnish with fresh parsley.

Chicken Mole (Mexico)

Ingredients:

- 4 bone-in chicken thighs
- 1 tablespoon vegetable oil
- 1 onion, chopped
- 2 cloves garlic, minced
- 1/4 cup cocoa powder
- 1 tablespoon chili powder
- 1 teaspoon ground cumin
- 1 teaspoon cinnamon
- 1/4 cup peanut butter
- 1/4 cup raisins
- 1 can (14 oz) diced tomatoes
- 1/2 cup chicken broth
- 1 tablespoon sugar
- Salt and pepper, to taste

Instructions:

1. Heat oil in a large pan over medium heat. Brown the chicken thighs on both sides and remove them from the pan.
2. In the same pan, sauté onion and garlic until softened.
3. Stir in cocoa powder, chili powder, cumin, cinnamon, peanut butter, raisins, tomatoes, chicken broth, and sugar. Bring to a simmer and cook for 10 minutes until the sauce thickens.
4. Return chicken to the pan and coat with the sauce. Cover and simmer for 30-40 minutes, until the chicken is tender.
5. Serve with rice or tortillas.

Peruvian Roast Chicken (Peru)

Ingredients:

- 4 bone-in chicken thighs
- 1/4 cup olive oil
- 3 cloves garlic, minced
- 1 tablespoon cumin
- 1 tablespoon paprika
- 1 tablespoon vinegar
- 1 tablespoon soy sauce
- 1 teaspoon ground turmeric
- Salt and pepper, to taste
- 1 lime, cut into wedges

Instructions:

1. Preheat oven to 400°F (200°C).
2. In a small bowl, combine olive oil, garlic, cumin, paprika, vinegar, soy sauce, turmeric, salt, and pepper. Rub the mixture onto the chicken thighs.
3. Place the chicken on a roasting pan and bake for 35-40 minutes, until the skin is crispy and the chicken is cooked through.
4. Serve with lime wedges and a side of potatoes or rice.

Chicken Paprikash (Hungary)

Ingredients:

- 4 bone-in chicken thighs or chicken breast
- 1 tablespoon olive oil
- 1 onion, chopped
- 2 tablespoons sweet paprika
- 1 teaspoon smoked paprika (optional)
- 1 bell pepper, sliced
- 1 cup chicken broth
- 1/2 cup sour cream
- 2 cloves garlic, minced
- Salt and pepper, to taste
- Fresh parsley, chopped (for garnish)

Instructions:

1. Heat olive oil in a large pot or Dutch oven over medium heat. Season the chicken with salt and pepper, then brown on both sides, about 6-8 minutes per side. Remove chicken from the pot.
2. In the same pot, sauté the onion and bell pepper until soft, about 5 minutes. Add garlic and paprika (both sweet and smoked) and cook for another 1-2 minutes until fragrant.
3. Return the chicken to the pot, add the chicken broth, and bring to a simmer. Cover and cook for 30-40 minutes, until the chicken is cooked through and tender.
4. Stir in sour cream, adjust seasoning, and simmer for an additional 5 minutes to thicken the sauce.
5. Serve over egg noodles, rice, or mashed potatoes, garnished with fresh parsley.

Chicken Souvlaki (Greece)

Ingredients:

- 4 boneless, skinless chicken breasts, cut into cubes
- 3 tablespoons olive oil
- 2 tablespoons lemon juice
- 2 teaspoons dried oregano
- 2 cloves garlic, minced
- 1 teaspoon ground cumin
- 1 teaspoon paprika
- Salt and pepper, to taste
- Pita bread, for serving
- Tzatziki sauce (for dipping)
- Fresh parsley, chopped (for garnish)

Instructions:

1. In a bowl, combine olive oil, lemon juice, oregano, garlic, cumin, paprika, salt, and pepper. Add the chicken cubes and marinate for at least 30 minutes (or up to overnight).
2. Preheat a grill or grill pan over medium-high heat. Thread the marinated chicken onto skewers.
3. Grill the chicken for 6-8 minutes, turning occasionally, until cooked through and slightly charred.
4. Serve the chicken skewers with pita bread, tzatziki sauce, and a garnish of fresh parsley.

Baked Chicken with Lemon and Herbs (France)

Ingredients:

- 4 bone-in, skinless chicken thighs
- 1 lemon, sliced
- 4 sprigs fresh rosemary
- 4 sprigs fresh thyme
- 2 tablespoons olive oil
- 3 cloves garlic, smashed
- Salt and pepper, to taste

Instructions:

1. Preheat oven to 400°F (200°C). Place chicken thighs in a baking dish.
2. Drizzle olive oil over the chicken and season with salt and pepper. Add the garlic, lemon slices, rosemary, and thyme around the chicken.
3. Bake for 35-45 minutes, until the chicken is golden brown and cooked through, with an internal temperature of 165°F (75°C).
4. Serve with roasted potatoes or a fresh salad.

Chicken Korma (India)

Ingredients:

- 4 boneless, skinless chicken breasts, cut into chunks
- 2 tablespoons vegetable oil
- 1 onion, chopped
- 2 cloves garlic, minced
- 1 tablespoon grated ginger
- 1 tablespoon ground cumin
- 1 tablespoon ground coriander
- 1 teaspoon ground turmeric
- 1 teaspoon garam masala
- 1/2 cup ground almonds
- 1 cup plain yogurt
- 1/2 cup coconut milk
- Salt, to taste
- Fresh cilantro, chopped (for garnish)

Instructions:

1. Heat oil in a large pan over medium heat. Add onions and cook until softened, about 5 minutes. Add garlic and ginger, cooking for an additional minute.
2. Stir in cumin, coriander, turmeric, and garam masala, cooking for 2 minutes until fragrant.
3. Add the chicken pieces and cook for 5-7 minutes until browned on all sides.
4. Stir in ground almonds, yogurt, and coconut milk, bringing the mixture to a simmer. Cook for 20-25 minutes until the chicken is tender and the sauce thickens.
5. Season with salt and garnish with fresh cilantro. Serve with basmati rice or naan bread.

Kung Pao Chicken (China)

Ingredients:

- 4 boneless, skinless chicken breasts, cubed
- 2 tablespoons soy sauce
- 1 tablespoon rice vinegar
- 1 tablespoon hoisin sauce
- 1 tablespoon sugar
- 1 teaspoon cornstarch
- 1/2 cup roasted peanuts
- 2 tablespoons vegetable oil
- 3 dried red chilies (optional)
- 2 cloves garlic, minced
- 1/2 bell pepper, chopped
- 1 small onion, chopped
- 1/4 cup green onions, sliced
- Salt, to taste

Instructions:

1. In a small bowl, whisk together soy sauce, rice vinegar, hoisin sauce, sugar, and cornstarch. Set aside.
2. Heat vegetable oil in a wok or large pan over medium-high heat. Add the dried chilies (if using), garlic, and bell pepper, stir-frying for 1-2 minutes.
3. Add the chicken and cook until browned and cooked through, about 5-7 minutes.
4. Add the sauce mixture to the pan, stirring to coat the chicken. Add the peanuts and cook for an additional 2-3 minutes, until the sauce thickens.
5. Garnish with green onions and serve with steamed rice.

Chicken Piri Piri (Portugal)

Ingredients:

- 4 bone-in, skinless chicken thighs
- 2 tablespoons olive oil
- 2 cloves garlic, minced
- 1 red chili, chopped (or 1 teaspoon chili flakes)
- 1 tablespoon paprika
- 1 tablespoon lemon juice
- 1 tablespoon red wine vinegar
- Salt and pepper, to taste

Instructions:

1. In a small bowl, mix olive oil, garlic, chili, paprika, lemon juice, red wine vinegar, salt, and pepper to create the marinade.
2. Coat the chicken with the marinade and refrigerate for at least 1 hour or overnight.
3. Preheat the grill or oven to medium-high heat. Grill or bake the chicken for 25-30 minutes, turning occasionally, until fully cooked and slightly charred.
4. Serve with rice or a salad.

Chicken Pot Pie (USA)

Ingredients:

- 2 cups cooked chicken, chopped
- 2 cups mixed vegetables (carrots, peas, corn)
- 1/4 cup butter
- 1/4 cup flour
- 2 cups chicken broth
- 1/2 cup milk
- 1/2 teaspoon dried thyme
- Salt and pepper, to taste
- 1 package pie crusts (or homemade crust)
- 1 egg, beaten (for egg wash)

Instructions:

1. Preheat oven to 400°F (200°C). Roll out the pie crust and line a 9-inch pie dish.
2. In a large saucepan, melt butter over medium heat. Stir in the flour to form a roux, then slowly whisk in chicken broth and milk. Bring to a simmer until the sauce thickens.
3. Add the chicken, vegetables, thyme, salt, and pepper. Stir to combine, then pour into the prepared pie dish.
4. Top with another pie crust, crimping the edges. Cut slits in the top to allow steam to escape.
5. Brush with egg wash and bake for 25-30 minutes, until golden brown. Let cool slightly before serving.

Chicken Empanadas (Argentina)

Ingredients:

- 2 cups cooked chicken, shredded
- 1 onion, chopped
- 2 tablespoons olive oil
- 1/2 cup green olives, chopped
- 1/4 cup raisins
- 1 teaspoon cumin
- 1 teaspoon paprika
- Salt and pepper, to taste
- 1 package empanada dough (store-bought or homemade)
- 1 egg, beaten (for egg wash)

Instructions:

1. In a pan, heat olive oil over medium heat. Sauté the onion until softened, about 5 minutes. Add the chicken, olives, raisins, cumin, paprika, salt, and pepper. Cook for 5 minutes, then remove from heat.
2. Preheat the oven to 375°F (190°C). Roll out the empanada dough and cut into circles.
3. Place a spoonful of the chicken mixture in the center of each dough circle. Fold and seal the edges by pressing with a fork.
4. Brush with beaten egg and bake for 20-25 minutes until golden brown.
5. Serve with a side of chimichurri sauce.

Chicken Schnitzel (Austria)

Ingredients:

- 4 boneless, skinless chicken breasts
- 1 cup all-purpose flour
- 2 large eggs, beaten
- 2 cups breadcrumbs (preferably panko)
- 1/2 cup vegetable oil (for frying)
- Salt and pepper, to taste
- Lemon wedges (for serving)
- Fresh parsley, chopped (for garnish)

Instructions:

1. Place the chicken breasts between two sheets of plastic wrap and gently pound with a meat mallet until about 1/2 inch thick.
2. Set up three shallow bowls: one with flour, one with beaten eggs, and one with breadcrumbs.
3. Season the chicken with salt and pepper, then dip each piece first in the flour, then the eggs, and finally the breadcrumbs, pressing down to coat evenly.
4. Heat oil in a large skillet over medium-high heat. Fry the chicken in batches, about 3-4 minutes per side, until golden brown and crispy.
5. Drain on paper towels and serve with lemon wedges and a sprinkle of fresh parsley.

Chicken Satay (Malaysia)

Ingredients:

- 4 boneless, skinless chicken thighs, cut into strips
- 2 tablespoons soy sauce
- 1 tablespoon brown sugar
- 2 tablespoons vegetable oil
- 1 tablespoon curry powder
- 1 teaspoon garlic powder
- 1 tablespoon lime juice
- Bamboo skewers (soaked in water for 30 minutes)

For Peanut Sauce:

- 1/2 cup peanut butter
- 2 tablespoons soy sauce
- 1 tablespoon brown sugar
- 1 tablespoon lime juice
- 1/2 cup coconut milk
- 1 teaspoon chili flakes (optional)

Instructions:

1. In a bowl, mix soy sauce, brown sugar, vegetable oil, curry powder, garlic powder, and lime juice. Add the chicken strips and marinate for at least 30 minutes.
2. Thread the chicken onto the soaked skewers.
3. Grill the chicken on a preheated grill or grill pan over medium heat for 4-5 minutes per side, until cooked through and slightly charred.
4. For the peanut sauce, whisk together peanut butter, soy sauce, brown sugar, lime juice, coconut milk, and chili flakes (if using) in a small saucepan. Heat over low heat until smooth.
5. Serve the chicken satay with the peanut sauce for dipping.

Chicken Enchiladas (Mexico)

Ingredients:

- 4 boneless, skinless chicken breasts, cooked and shredded
- 1 can (14 oz) red enchilada sauce
- 1 cup shredded cheddar cheese
- 1 cup shredded mozzarella cheese
- 10-12 corn tortillas
- 1 small onion, chopped
- 1 tablespoon olive oil
- 1/2 teaspoon ground cumin
- 1/2 teaspoon garlic powder
- Salt and pepper, to taste
- Fresh cilantro, chopped (for garnish)

Instructions:

1. Preheat oven to 375°F (190°C).
2. Heat olive oil in a skillet over medium heat and sauté the onion until softened, about 5 minutes. Add the shredded chicken, cumin, garlic powder, salt, and pepper. Stir to combine and cook for an additional 2-3 minutes.
3. In a shallow bowl, pour a little enchilada sauce. Dip each tortilla into the sauce to coat, then fill with the chicken mixture and a sprinkle of cheese. Roll up the tortillas and place seam-side down in a greased baking dish.
4. Pour the remaining enchilada sauce over the top of the rolled tortillas and sprinkle with the remaining cheese.
5. Bake for 20 minutes, until the cheese is melted and bubbly. Garnish with fresh cilantro before serving.

Chicken Piccata (Italy)

Ingredients:

- 4 boneless, skinless chicken breasts
- 1/2 cup all-purpose flour
- 1/4 cup olive oil
- 1/4 cup white wine
- 2 tablespoons lemon juice
- 1/4 cup capers, drained
- 2 tablespoons butter
- Fresh parsley, chopped (for garnish)
- Salt and pepper, to taste

Instructions:

1. Season the chicken breasts with salt and pepper. Dredge each piece in flour, shaking off the excess.
2. In a large skillet, heat olive oil over medium heat. Cook the chicken for 3-4 minutes per side, until golden brown and cooked through. Remove the chicken from the skillet and set aside.
3. In the same skillet, add white wine, lemon juice, and capers. Bring to a simmer, scraping the bottom of the pan to release any browned bits.
4. Stir in butter to create a smooth sauce. Return the chicken to the skillet and spoon the sauce over the top.
5. Garnish with fresh parsley and serve with pasta or rice.

Chicken Rendang (Indonesia)

Ingredients:

- 4 boneless, skinless chicken thighs, cut into pieces
- 1 tablespoon vegetable oil
- 1 onion, chopped
- 2 cloves garlic, minced
- 1 tablespoon grated ginger
- 2 tablespoons curry powder
- 1 can (14 oz) coconut milk
- 1/4 cup beef broth or water
- 2 tablespoons soy sauce
- 2 tablespoons brown sugar
- 1 cinnamon stick
- 3-4 kaffir lime leaves (optional)
- Salt, to taste
- Fresh cilantro, chopped (for garnish)

Instructions:

1. In a large pot, heat the vegetable oil over medium heat. Sauté the onion, garlic, and ginger until softened, about 5 minutes.
2. Add curry powder and cook for another 1-2 minutes, until fragrant.
3. Add the chicken pieces and cook until browned on all sides, about 5 minutes.
4. Pour in the coconut milk, beef broth, soy sauce, brown sugar, cinnamon stick, and kaffir lime leaves. Bring to a simmer.
5. Reduce heat to low and cook for 45-60 minutes, until the sauce has thickened and the chicken is tender.
6. Season with salt to taste, and garnish with fresh cilantro before serving.

Chicken Caesar Salad (USA)

Ingredients:

- 2 boneless, skinless chicken breasts
- 4 cups Romaine lettuce, chopped
- 1/2 cup Caesar dressing
- 1/2 cup grated Parmesan cheese
- Croutons, for topping
- Salt and pepper, to taste

Instructions:

1. Season the chicken breasts with salt and pepper. Grill or pan-fry them over medium heat for 5-7 minutes per side, until cooked through.
2. Let the chicken rest for a few minutes before slicing it thinly.
3. In a large bowl, toss the chopped Romaine lettuce with Caesar dressing and grated Parmesan cheese.
4. Top with sliced chicken and croutons, and serve immediately.

Poulet Roti (France)

Ingredients:

- 1 whole chicken (about 4-5 lbs)
- 2 tablespoons olive oil
- 2 cloves garlic, minced
- 1 lemon, halved
- 2 sprigs fresh rosemary
- Salt and pepper, to taste

Instructions:

1. Preheat oven to 425°F (220°C).
2. Season the chicken generously with salt and pepper, both inside and out. Stuff the cavity with lemon halves and rosemary sprigs.
3. Rub the outside of the chicken with olive oil and minced garlic.
4. Place the chicken on a rack in a roasting pan and roast for 1-1.5 hours, or until the internal temperature reaches 165°F (75°C).
5. Let the chicken rest for 10 minutes before carving. Serve with roasted vegetables or potatoes.

Khao Man Gai (Thailand)

Ingredients:

- 4 bone-in, skinless chicken thighs
- 2 cups jasmine rice, rinsed
- 4 cups chicken broth
- 2 cloves garlic, minced
- 1 tablespoon ginger, minced
- 2 tablespoons vegetable oil
- 1 tablespoon soy sauce
- 1 tablespoon fish sauce
- 1 cucumber, sliced (for garnish)
- Fresh cilantro, chopped (for garnish)

Instructions:

1. In a large pot, heat the vegetable oil and sauté the garlic and ginger until fragrant, about 2 minutes.
2. Add the chicken thighs to the pot and cook for 5-6 minutes per side, until browned.
3. Add the rice to the pot, followed by the chicken broth, soy sauce, and fish sauce. Bring to a simmer.
4. Cover and cook for 20 minutes, until the rice is tender and the chicken is cooked through.
5. Remove the chicken, shred it, and serve over the rice. Garnish with cucumber slices and fresh cilantro.

Spicy Chicken Wings (Korea)

Ingredients:

- 12 chicken wings, separated into drumettes and flats
- 1 tablespoon vegetable oil
- 1/4 cup soy sauce
- 1 tablespoon rice vinegar
- 2 tablespoons gochujang (Korean chili paste)
- 1 tablespoon honey
- 2 cloves garlic, minced
- 1 teaspoon ginger, minced
- 1 teaspoon sesame oil
- 2 tablespoons sesame seeds (for garnish)
- Green onions, chopped (for garnish)

Instructions:

1. Preheat oven to 400°F (200°C). Line a baking sheet with parchment paper.
2. Season the chicken wings with salt and pepper. Heat vegetable oil in a large skillet over medium-high heat and sear the wings for 2-3 minutes per side, until golden brown.
3. Transfer the wings to the prepared baking sheet and bake for 25-30 minutes until crispy and cooked through.
4. In a small saucepan, combine soy sauce, rice vinegar, gochujang, honey, garlic, ginger, and sesame oil. Bring to a simmer and cook for 3-4 minutes until the sauce thickens slightly.
5. Toss the baked wings in the spicy sauce, then garnish with sesame seeds and chopped green onions.

Chicken Paella (Spain)

Ingredients:

- 4 bone-in, skinless chicken thighs
- 1 tablespoon olive oil
- 1 onion, chopped
- 2 cloves garlic, minced
- 1 red bell pepper, chopped
- 1 1/2 cups short-grain rice (like Arborio or paella rice)
- 1/2 teaspoon saffron threads (optional)
- 3 cups chicken broth
- 1/2 cup white wine
- 1 cup frozen peas
- 1/2 teaspoon paprika
- Salt and pepper, to taste
- Lemon wedges (for serving)

Instructions:

1. Heat olive oil in a large pan or paella pan over medium heat. Brown the chicken thighs for 5-6 minutes per side, then remove them from the pan and set aside.
2. In the same pan, sauté the onion, garlic, and bell pepper until softened, about 5 minutes.
3. Stir in the rice and paprika, and cook for 1-2 minutes. Add the saffron (if using), chicken broth, and white wine, then bring to a simmer.
4. Return the chicken thighs to the pan, skin-side up. Cover and cook on low heat for 25-30 minutes, until the rice is tender and the chicken is cooked through.
5. Add the peas and cook for an additional 5 minutes. Season with salt and pepper, and serve with lemon wedges.

Chicken Adobo (Philippines)

Ingredients:

- 4 bone-in, skinless chicken thighs
- 1/4 cup soy sauce
- 1/4 cup vinegar
- 1 onion, sliced
- 4 cloves garlic, smashed
- 2 bay leaves
- 1/2 teaspoon black peppercorns
- 1 tablespoon vegetable oil
- 1 tablespoon brown sugar
- 1/2 cup water
- Cooked rice (for serving)

Instructions:

1. In a large bowl, combine soy sauce, vinegar, onion, garlic, bay leaves, peppercorns, and sugar. Add the chicken and marinate for at least 1 hour.
2. Heat oil in a large skillet over medium-high heat. Add the chicken and brown on all sides for 5-6 minutes.
3. Add the marinade and water to the skillet, and bring to a simmer. Cover and cook for 30 minutes, until the chicken is tender and cooked through.
4. Remove the chicken from the skillet, and simmer the sauce for an additional 10-15 minutes until thickened.
5. Serve the chicken adobo with steamed rice and the sauce.

Chicken Burritos (Mexico)

Ingredients:

- 2 boneless, skinless chicken breasts
- 1 tablespoon olive oil
- 1 packet taco seasoning
- 1/2 cup salsa
- 4 flour tortillas
- 1 cup shredded cheese (cheddar or Mexican blend)
- 1/2 cup sour cream
- 1/4 cup chopped cilantro
- 1/2 cup guacamole
- Lettuce, chopped (for garnish)

Instructions:

1. Season the chicken breasts with taco seasoning. Heat olive oil in a skillet over medium heat and cook the chicken for 6-7 minutes per side until fully cooked. Shred the chicken with a fork.
2. In the same skillet, add the salsa to the shredded chicken and cook for an additional 2-3 minutes.
3. Warm the flour tortillas in a dry skillet or microwave. Spoon the chicken mixture onto the center of each tortilla, then top with cheese, sour cream, cilantro, and guacamole.
4. Roll up the burritos, folding in the sides, and serve with extra salsa and lettuce.

Chicken Vindaloo (India)

Ingredients:

- 4 bone-in, skinless chicken thighs, cut into pieces
- 2 tablespoons vegetable oil
- 1 onion, chopped
- 4 cloves garlic, minced
- 1 tablespoon ginger, minced
- 1 tablespoon ground cumin
- 1 tablespoon ground turmeric
- 1 tablespoon garam masala
- 1 teaspoon ground coriander
- 2 tablespoons white vinegar
- 1 can (14 oz) diced tomatoes
- 1/2 cup water
- 1/2 teaspoon red chili flakes (optional)
- Fresh cilantro, chopped (for garnish)
- Cooked rice (for serving)

Instructions:

1. Heat the vegetable oil in a large pot over medium heat. Add the onion and sauté until softened, about 5 minutes.
2. Stir in the garlic, ginger, cumin, turmeric, garam masala, and coriander. Cook for 1-2 minutes until fragrant.
3. Add the chicken pieces and cook for 5 minutes, turning occasionally to brown on all sides.
4. Pour in the vinegar, tomatoes, water, and red chili flakes (if using). Bring to a simmer and cook for 30 minutes until the chicken is tender and the sauce thickens.
5. Garnish with fresh cilantro and serve with rice.

Chicken and Chorizo Paella (Spain)

Ingredients:

- 2 boneless, skinless chicken thighs, cut into pieces
- 1/2 pound chorizo sausage, sliced
- 1 tablespoon olive oil
- 1 onion, chopped
- 2 cloves garlic, minced
- 1 bell pepper, chopped
- 1 1/2 cups short-grain rice
- 1/2 teaspoon saffron threads (optional)
- 3 cups chicken broth
- 1/2 cup white wine
- 1/2 cup frozen peas
- Lemon wedges (for serving)

Instructions:

1. Heat olive oil in a large pan or paella pan over medium heat. Brown the chicken pieces and chorizo sausage for 5-6 minutes, then remove from the pan and set aside.
2. In the same pan, sauté the onion, garlic, and bell pepper until softened, about 5 minutes.
3. Stir in the rice and saffron, then add the chicken broth and white wine. Bring to a simmer.
4. Return the chicken and chorizo to the pan and cook, uncovered, for 20-25 minutes, until the rice is tender and the liquid is absorbed.
5. Stir in the peas and cook for an additional 5 minutes. Serve with lemon wedges.

Stuffed Chicken with Spinach and Feta (Greece)

Ingredients:

- 4 boneless, skinless chicken breasts
- 1 cup fresh spinach, chopped
- 1/2 cup crumbled feta cheese
- 2 cloves garlic, minced
- 1 tablespoon olive oil
- 1/4 teaspoon dried oregano
- Salt and pepper, to taste

Instructions:

1. Preheat oven to 375°F (190°C).
2. Cut a pocket in each chicken breast by slicing horizontally but not all the way through.
3. In a bowl, combine spinach, feta, and garlic. Stuff each chicken breast with the mixture, then secure with toothpicks.
4. Heat olive oil in a skillet over medium-high heat. Sear the chicken for 3-4 minutes per side until browned.
5. Transfer the chicken to the oven and bake for 20-25 minutes until cooked through. Season with salt, pepper, and oregano.

Cacciatore di Pollo (Italy)

Ingredients:

- 4 bone-in, skinless chicken thighs
- 1 tablespoon olive oil
- 1 onion, chopped
- 2 cloves garlic, minced
- 1 red bell pepper, chopped
- 1 can (14 oz) diced tomatoes
- 1/2 cup dry white wine
- 1/2 cup chicken broth
- 2 tablespoons capers
- 1 teaspoon dried oregano
- Salt and pepper, to taste
- Fresh basil, chopped (for garnish)

Instructions:

1. Heat olive oil in a large skillet over medium heat. Brown the chicken thighs on both sides for 5-6 minutes per side. Remove and set aside.
2. In the same skillet, sauté the onion, garlic, and bell pepper until softened, about 5 minutes.
3. Add the tomatoes, wine, chicken broth, capers, and oregano. Bring to a simmer.
4. Return the chicken to the pan, cover, and cook for 25-30 minutes until the chicken is cooked through and tender.
5. Garnish with fresh basil and serve with pasta or crusty bread.

Grilled Peri Peri Chicken (South Africa)

Ingredients:

- 4 boneless, skinless chicken breasts
- 1/4 cup olive oil
- 1/4 cup lemon juice
- 2 tablespoons peri peri sauce (or hot sauce)
- 2 cloves garlic, minced
- 1 tablespoon paprika
- 1 teaspoon dried oregano
- Salt and pepper, to taste

Instructions:

1. In a bowl, mix olive oil, lemon juice, peri peri sauce, garlic, paprika, oregano, salt, and pepper.
2. Coat the chicken breasts in the marinade and let them sit for at least 30 minutes.
3. Preheat the grill to medium-high heat. Grill the chicken for 6-7 minutes per side, until cooked through.
4. Serve with a side of grilled vegetables or rice.

Chicken Szechuan (China)

Ingredients:

- 2 boneless, skinless chicken breasts, thinly sliced
- 1 tablespoon vegetable oil
- 1 onion, sliced
- 2 cloves garlic, minced
- 2 tablespoons soy sauce
- 2 tablespoons rice vinegar
- 1 tablespoon Szechuan peppercorns
- 1/2 teaspoon crushed red pepper flakes
- 1 tablespoon hoisin sauce
- 1 tablespoon sesame oil
- 1/4 cup water
- Chopped green onions (for garnish)

Instructions:

1. Heat vegetable oil in a wok or large skillet over medium-high heat. Cook the chicken slices for 5-6 minutes, until browned and cooked through.
2. Add onion and garlic and sauté for 2 minutes.
3. Stir in soy sauce, rice vinegar, Szechuan peppercorns, red pepper flakes, hoisin sauce, and sesame oil. Add water and cook for another 3-4 minutes.
4. Garnish with green onions and serve with rice or noodles.